© 2006 Assouline Publishing
601 West 26th Street, 18th floor
New York, NY 10001, USA
Tel.: 212 989-6810   Fax: 212 647-0005
www.assouline.com

ISBN: 2 84323 870 6

Color separation: Gravor (Switzerland)
Printed by Grafiche Milani (Italy)

ÉLISABETH VÉDRENNE

BISAZZA

CONTEMPORARY MOSAICS

ASSOULINE

The magic of mosaic

t he first time I happened to see Bisazza mosaics was in Venice, in a minute apartment like most apartments in La Serenissima that aren't lucky enough to be palaces. To push back its walls, its owners had enlisted the services of a talented architect, who had transformed it into a casket the color of the waters of the lagoon.

It was filled with the shimmer of the turquoise gloss paint and gold mosaics that had redrawn the space and created new perspectives. Like Ariadne's golden thread, the mosaics led one off on a treasure hunt, drawing an imaginary labyrinth on the floor, climbing up the walls, zigzagging through display cases full of glassware, crossing the tops of pieces of furniture, continually prolonging surfaces.

The architect, I discovered, had used Bisazza gold mosaic. Like a couturier oversewing his client to create a garment, he had transformed a small, low-ceilinged space into a marvelous liquid box in which one had the illusion of walking into a chasm. I learned a lot that day about the enchanting power mosaic can exercise over architecture, about its capacities to remodel and embellish the banal, to create illusion, to enchant both inside and out. Yet since the dawn of time we have known that these tiny, modest little cubes, these glass, marble or stone *tesserae*, can transform the surface of a floor, wall or monument. I also understood that the omnipotence of the architect or designer is rivaled only by that of the manufacturer, that key person whose responsibility it is to invent materials, color ranges, shapes, sizes and, most important of all, quality. Mosaic today has to adapt to the speed of the world. It has to be lighter, more durable, easier to use and even more seductive. Only Bisazza has all these qualities.

Reconciling art and industry

bisazza is the only mosaic house in the world with experience both in traditional, handmade mosaic and the most innovative industrial manufacturing techniques. I say "house" because to my mind Bisazza is every bit the equal of the Italian couture houses that have come to epitomize Italian style, houses whose own brilliant mix of dazzling ancestral craft and a highly contemporary approach ensures they evolve and survive. They are characterized as much by their technical excellence as their communication skills. With their dynamism, sense of mobility and the creativity of their design studios, these Italian houses, often family businesses, have not contented themselves with merely inheriting but have known how to adapt and take risks while keeping a cool head. With stubbornness and pragmatism, they have forced industry to adapt to their creativity. And thanks to Bisazza, what is true in the worlds of fashion, leather goods, fabrics and furniture also goes for mosaic.

How, in only fifty years, does one transform a small mosaic factory into a veritable luxury industry? It all began in the magic triangle between Vicenza, Venice and Trieste. This region, once the granary and larder of La Serenissima but which in the nineteenth century became so poor its inhabitants emigrated en masse, is now one of the most industrious and dynamic regions in Italy. Renato Bisazza, from the Vicenza area, enterprising, inquisitive, an art lover but full of common sense, was intent on moving with the spirit of the time. He noticed, in the post-war climate that triggered the economic boom in Italy in the late Fifties, that there was a revival in taste for Venetian glass, and that this had inevitably led to a renewed interest in a completely forgotten technique, glass mosaic. The mosaic industry had all but died out, the mosaicists in Ravenna and Venice could be counted on one hand, but further north, in Friuli, the Mosaic School at Spilimbergo had reopened. The school had been created in the Twenties expressly to train artists capable of using mosaic as it was in Roman times, and in so doing soften and enliven the walls of the pompous buildings of Mussolini's regime.

Renato Bisazza sensed a revival of this ancestral craft and anticipated a real demand for it. In 1956, he and his brother created a factory producing mosaic by hand at first but which soon adopted semi-industrial techniques. And it worked. He improved the traditional cubes of glass paste or smalt, perfected his production of glass enamel, aventurine and gold, widened their color range, and could thus again cover the bottoms of swimming pools and beautiful "American-style" bathrooms that the new Italian consumer society dreamt of. In short, he restored the prestige of mosaic in the Italian home.

New challenges

he was soon joined by his son Piero Bisazza, who in the late 1980s persuaded him to change course by inviting the architect Alessandro Mendini to come and work at the company and advise them artistically. The choice of Mendini was a trendy initiative and a daring premonition. Mendini and his *Studio Alchemia*, like Sottsass Jr and his *Memphis* group, was a leading representative of the new, radical, joyful and playful Italian design. Neither bourgeois or conformist, he would profoundly change things at Bisazza by giving the company a slightly zany image tinged with avant-gardism, and at any rate utterly contemporary.

The difficulty for a mosaic manufacturer is not to get bogged down in the clichés inherent in a craft with such a prestigious past. Piero Bisazza was immediately aware of this stumbling block. With acute foresight, he analyzed the mosaic industry's situation and challenges. His contemporary art collector's eye also served him in good stead. Completely in tune with his generation and his time, he addressed the dilemma of his trade: how to successfully dust off its tradition without removing the very tradition it is based on? How to awaken the desire of contemporary buyers without merely reproducing – albeit perfectly –the time-proven recipes of yesteryear?

Few are the visitors who do not marvel at the trompe-l'oeil effects of the Byzantine mosaics in the Basilica di San Vitale in Ravenna. Who would not tremble at the sight of the enormous, shimmering mosaic waves of the Deluge in the Basilica San Marco? And who has not admired how the Ancient Romans, such remarkable architects, revolutionized interior architecture throughout the Mediterranean basin with the mosaics of friezes, bands and innumerable geometric motifs with which they decorated their floors and terraces?

Everyone has dreamt of having mosaics like that in their own home, and this is exactly what Bisazza set out to do: to realize that dream within the context of our modern, daily lives, not by harking back to ancient times but in pixels on a giant screen enlarged by our modern vision and even that of the future.

All these motifs, those derived from them and those we haven't yet even dreamt of, the infinite varieties of bouquets, giant flowers, jewels of variable geometry, undulating waves, wall hangings, finery, fabrics, folds, stars, etc., they are all there in the Bisazza catalogue.

They have been adapted to our twenty-first-century vision, to today's taste for stylistic "sampling," pastiche and interbreeding, and our contemporary appetite for extremes, excess, the most and least, the rococo and the minimal, fantasy and austerity, stylistic affectedness and monastic simplicity, the multicolored and the gray, the kitsch and the tasteful.

Bisazza will try anything: a black and white Greek design, a giant beige chevron motif à la David Hicks, a wall of coral, leopard or giraffe skin around a bath, or a bedroom entirely in gold. Whatever you want... Every client should be able to satisfy his or her most classical or unconventional desires in this Ali Baba's cave full of everything one could possibly want or imagine one wanted.

Mendini magic

alessandro Mendini immediately understood the myriad possibilities of such a cave and, poetic Aladdin that he is, didn't hesitate to rummage around in it. What he found largely responded to the challenges Piero Bisazza wanted to address. With his characteristic professionalism, he placed his vision of the world in the service of Bisazza and in doing so enriched it. He brought with him the passion for Pointillism he had inherited from the Italian Futurists, his unbridled fantasy, adding to the natural kaleidoscope of Bisazza mosaics "un certain je ne sais quoi" that other manufacturers lacked. Mendini was already a star, and his facetious, smiling figures had been a huge hit in another company then in full expansion: Alessi. For Bisazza, he invented a new language, a profoundly optimist, Utopian world. He imbued Bisazza's simple, modest cubes of sand, silicates and oxides with spiritual powers. He illuminated the world of mosaic from the inside, and in so doing propelled the company into the contemporary spotlight. He and his research studio created the *Neomosaico* Collection, giving Bisazza the possibility of creating magical interiors. Its sparkling colors and mixtures scored a direct hit and his eclecticism convinced the most skeptical.

Mendini adores youth and surrounded himself with a whole generation of enthusiastic designers who used Bisazza's multicolored cubes to cover furniture, walls, objects in innovative ways. He revolutionized Bisazza's hitherto conservative, rather staid image, injecting it with pep and audacity.

In Mendini, Piero Bisazza found a master, heeded his advice and kept his constant desire for a positive beauty in which memory and inventiveness can cohabit, and in which pragmatism does not preclude the spirit of adventure. Out of this collaboration came several masterpieces: the spiral staircase trickling like a fountain of color in the museum in Groningen in Holland, the metro stations in Naples, the sparks of poetry in the garden of the Fondation Cartier in Paris (*Pot pour le Cèdre*, 2002), and the admirable *Mobili da Uomo* sculptures (1997), "manservants" in the form of giant Pop objects entirely sheathed with gold, tutelary figures permanently keeping watch over the showroom at Alte's head office.

Discovering the world

Piero Bisazza is a hive of focused activity and is undoubtedly still inspired by the Mendini philosophy in his constant quest to improve productivity and quality, technique and form. Condemned by the implacable law of globalization to seek business ever further afield, having conquered the italian market, he went to discover America. He realized that he had to do away with his cramped, uninviting retail outlets and lure customers into showcases conceived as boutiques and designed by the greatest architects.

He had to invent the event, and began in that climate so ideally suited for mosaics, in the land of David Hockney's sparkling swimming pools, California. A study of the Miami market followed in 1992 and a memorable showroom was opened in New York. The Americans proved avid consumers of Bisazza's little cubes of happiness. New research workshops were created and great progress was made in those fields so crucial to any luxury industry today, marketing and distribution. Meanwhile, in Europe, a showroom was opened in Milan and is regularly metamorphosed with each new fashion. Barcelona followed suit, then Berlin, then London. Most of them were all sensuous curves, designed by Fabio Novembre. In 2006, it was Paris's turn, in very sophisticated tones of gold and silver signed by Carlo Dal Bianco, whom we also owe the enormous pale button roses on a black ground that welcome to Alte's headquarters near Vicenza. The effect is spectacular, the surprise guaranteed, one's senses awakened, one's appetite stimulated...

Bisazza has offices and branches all over the world, from Australia to China, through India, Russia, Spain and England. Piero Bisazza takes as much care over his sales force as he does his image. It was he who enlarged and redecorated the showroom of the company in Alte. On the same site he built an ultra-modern and incredibly aesthetic factory. Nothing was neglected. Employees and mosaicists, glass blowers and technicians, scientists and designers mingle in gray and black hangars heightened with bright yellow pipe work, to the background noise of truck drivers' shouts and the cascading tinkle of shattering glass. Every detail was pondered over, right down to the colors of the plastic bins – vivid red or emerald green depending on their use. Piero Bisazza has an infallible instinct and his acute sense of realism would be useless without the intuition which constantly guides him to the most unconventional solutions.

Sexy mosaic!

to replace Mendini was no easy matter. The choice of the very young designer Fabio Novembre was a radical one and proved to be a huge success. Bisazza went into orbit around this young mad dog bubbling over with ideas, sensuality and theatricality. The Alte showroom was filled with mountains of breaking waves, corridors with voluptuous female forms, mottled blues and baroque red made a comeback, stripes crinkled and warped, and mosaic began shamelessly and unrestrainedly undulating and folding like baroque drapery. A new page had been turned. Bisazza had made its entry into the world of ostentatious luxury of the discothèques and bars, and sumptuous hotels where dreamlike women mingle in the labyrinths of gynoecium-like swimming pools. The change could seem brutal, this new universe too flamboyant, too brash, the image excessive, overdone. But it has been a huge success.

Once again, Piero Bisazza perfectly analyzed and understood the communication mechanisms at work at the chaotic end of the twentieth century. He invented sexy mosaic! He was joined by his sister Rossella Bisazza in the communication department, a woman whose exquisite appearance and charm are equaled only by the unfailing energy of the ballerina she once was. He copied the methods of the fashion world, showing his wares in the most improbable venues and to most vertiginous music. He understood that there comes a point when, like the couturiers, one has to create entertainment, sell to the rhythm of the "seasons."

And yet again, it worked. Just like Dior's clients don't go to Dior boutiques to buy Galliano's powdered wigs, Bisazza's clients are entitled to enjoy its striped universes with golden plumage and silver lamps even if they do only come out of its boutiques with the equivalent of the ever-fashionable "little black dress," enough to cover their bathroom and perhaps their hallway in dove gray. Piero Bisazza made his entry into a luxurious and fragile world in which one has to please people all over the world whilst remaining faithful to one's company's traditions and one's own personal convictions – a balancing act in which it isn't enough to know how to walk along a rope elegantly. Piero Bisazza is therefore a man in a hurry, perpetually on the edge, excessively reactive, alert to the slightest scent and ever-ready to explore a new direction.

A contemporary vision

He was therefore immediately seduced by the approach of the Dutch designer Marcel Wanders, his fresh, by caustic manner nurtured in the Nineties with the Dutch group Droog Design, by his art of the explosive cocktail and sense irony perfectly suited to the dawn of the twenty-first century. His approach to the banality, absurdity and anxiety of our old western society through humor was brilliant. Wanders brought with him in his luggage the stereotyped craft imagery of our grandmothers, huge naïve flowers, needlepoint tapestry, lace, crochet, ceramics and sundry other old ladies' frills and flounces, in short, everything that would have been merely supremely kitsch without his intervention. He invented the concept of funny poetry. He had already presented his famous magic pebbles covered with large naïve flowers. And he has just lined the interiors of the mythical *Lute Suites* hotel near Amsterdam with Bisazza mosaic, a fine example of contemporary total art. His ability to reconcile opposites, associate the distant and recent past, and create multiple viewpoints to get us to laugh at ourselves was new form of positive art that couldn't leave Piero Bisazza indifferent.

With Wanders, as with Andrée Putman, Oscar Tusquets, Javier Mariscal and many other designers of all nationalities, Bisazza seems to be gravitating towards a new serenity. Patricia Urquiola, the new star of the Milan scene, and also Marco Braga and Carlo Dal Bianco, have entered the Piero Bisazza sphere. A new era is beginning, and there is no reason why it shouldn't work. Bisazza knows every intricacy of the mechanisms which enable him to preserve the collective memory and knowledge that has generated the word "mosaic," whilst superimposing on it the absolutely modern images which that tradition has generated over the last fifty years. Year after year it continues to construct a very fluid, flexible universe in which, like a great chef, it blends past, present and future. The Bisazza style is just that: a mosaic of mosaics in perpetual mutation.

Bisazza is a moving, living, mutating organism, like a tree which has beautiful, classical harmonious branches, but also more mischievous and funny ones here and there, branches spiced with wilder perfumes or, on the contrary, with more delicate ones, and of course laden with golden fruits and leaves, as in the Garden of Eden.

One can sum up the talent of Bisazza in a single feat: to have transformed a humble glass tessera with no other ambition than to be a mere construction material, into a tool capable of capturing the spirit of the times.

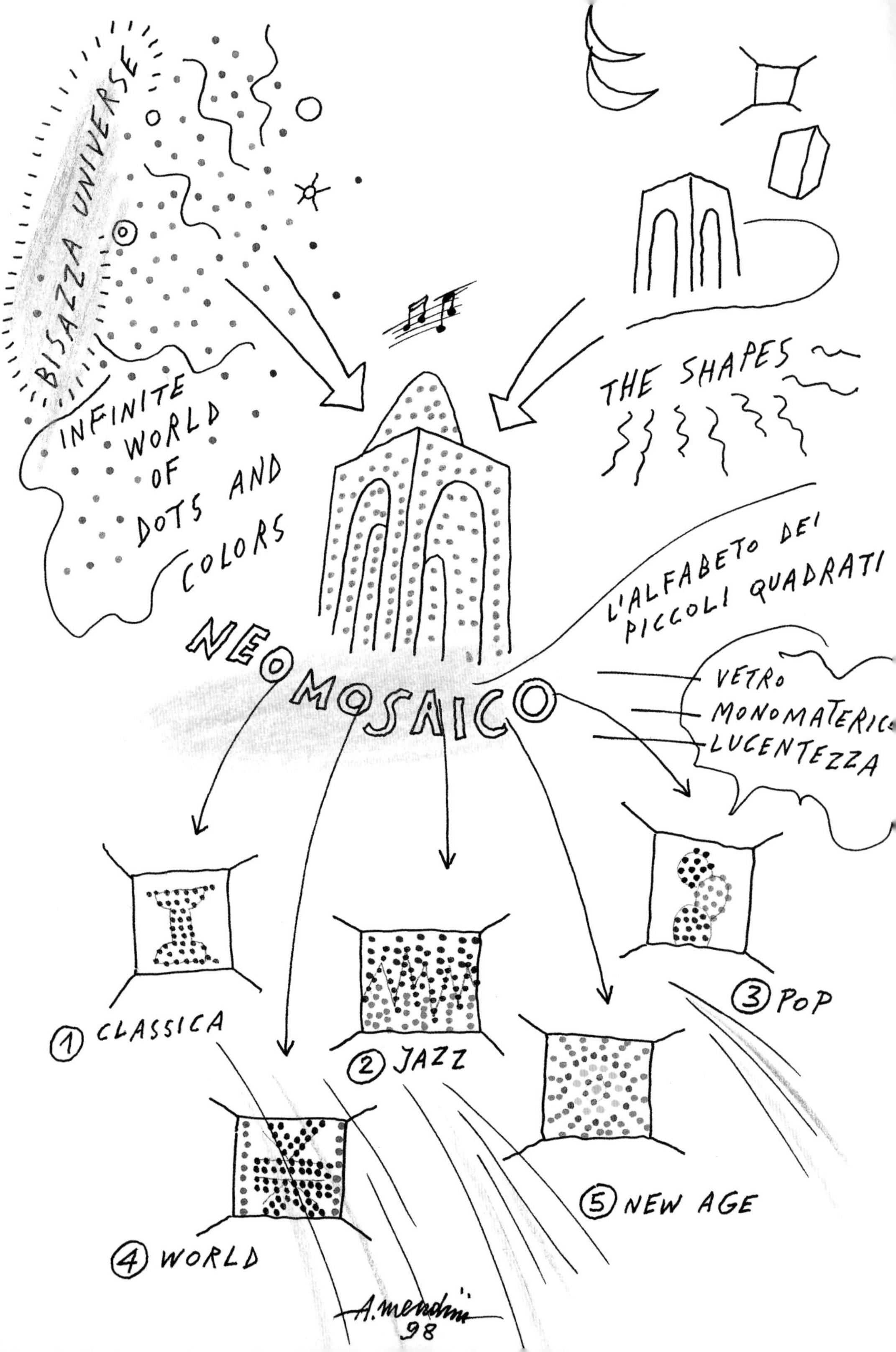

BISAZZA UNIVERSE

INFINITE WORLD OF DOTS AND COLORS

THE SHAPES

NEOMOSAICO

L'ALFABETO DEI PICCOLI QUADRATI

VETRO
MONOMATERIC·
LUCENTEZZA

① CLASSICA

② JAZZ

③ POP

④ WORLD

⑤ NEW AGE

A. mendini
98

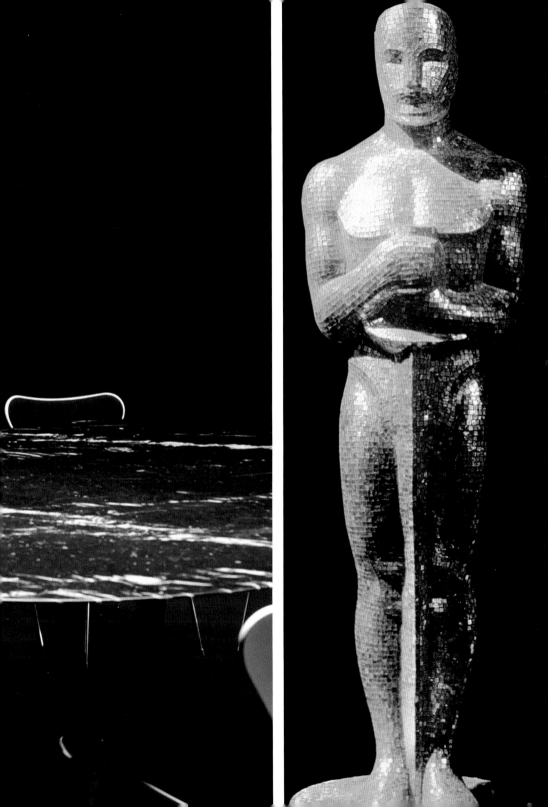

LES BALLETS RUSSES À L'OPÉRA

KANDINSKY

PIET MONDRIAN

TIZIANO

CAAR DESIGN

MODERN GLAMOUR

ENCOUNTERS

THE ART OF THE
CIGAR LABEL

AMERICAN PHOTOGRAPHY

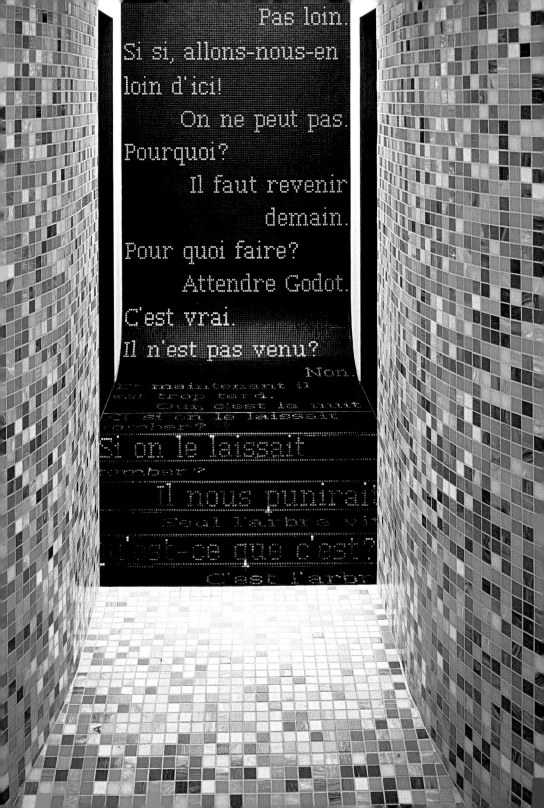

Pas loin.

Si si, allons-nous-en
loin d'ici!

On ne peut pas.

Pourquoi?

Il faut revenir
demain.

Pour quoi faire?

Attendre Godot.

C'est vrai.

Il n'est pas venu?

Non.

Et maintenant il
est trop tard.

Oui, c'est la nuit.
Et si on le laissait
tomber?

Si on le laissait
tomber?

Il nous punirait.

Seul l'arbre vit.

Qu'est-ce que c'est?

C'est l'arbre.

Chronology

1956:	Renato Bisazza founds Vetricolor at Alte, Vicenza, Italy.
1960s:	Numerous exterior mosaics for facades and urban spaces in Italy and abroad. Perfection of the form of the bevelled tessera (increased adhesion and more pleasant to the touch) and technical research to increase production capacity.
1970s:	Development of foreign markets in Africa, the Middle East and the Far East, notably with the realisation of splendid mosques with golden cupolas and the facades of huge edifices.
1972-1973:	The old gas ovens are replaced with electric continuous heat furnaces to enable the transition to industrial glass paste production.
1980-1985:	First use of computer generated techniques in mosaic fresco design.
1988:	*Torre Paradiso*, Hiroshima, Japan: the first project for which Alessandro Mendini uses Bisazza mosaic.
1989:	Vetricolor changes its name to Bisazza.
1990s:	Mosaic begins to be used by interior designers. Bisazza broadens its product and color range.
1994:	Opening of the Blumarine shop in London, Fabio Novembre's first project entirely in Bisazza mosaic.
1995:	Opening of Bisazza subsidiaries in the United States, India and Hong Kong.
1996-1999:	Alessandro Mendini is appointed Bisazza's artistic director.
1996:	September: Mendini organises the "Artinmosaico" exhibition in Naples, with the participation of important Italian and international designers.
2000:	January: Piero Bisazza becomes CEO of the group.
2000-2001:	Opening of subsidiaries in France, the United Kingdom, Spain, the Philippines and Australia. Fabio Novembre is appointed artistic director.
2002:	Opening of subsidiaries in Germany and Russia. April: opening of a Bisazza showroom in Milan.
2003:	October: opening of a Bisazza showroom in New York. November: opening of a Bisazza showroom in Berlin.
2004:	Creation of the Bisazza Design Studio to coordinate the collections and lines of the Bisazza spaces worldwide. Inauguration of a subsidiary in China.
2005:	September: opening of a Bisazza showroom in London.
2006:	March: opening of a Bisazza showroom in Paris. September: opening of a Bisazza showroom in Barcelona.

Four tailored outfits for an emblematic car. "Mini wears Bisazza" project, presented at the Salone del Mobile, Milano, 2005.
© *Ottavio Tomasini, 2005.*

BISAZZA

This *Étoiles Oro Giallo* décor is a subtle mix of gold and glass tesserae. Design: Carlo Dal Bianco. Also available in a silvery *Oro Bianco* version. Stylist: Miguel Arnau. © Giampaolo Sgura, 2005.

Lampada, by Alessandro Mendini for the "Mobili da Uomo" collection, in which the golden giant objects seem to come from an Alice in Designland world. © Alberto Ferrero, 2002.
Another majestic world with its golden mosaics: the bathroom Art Deco created by Jacques-Émile Ruhlman in 1937 for the ministère des Affaires Étrangères in Paris. © Guillaume de Laubier.

Entrance hall of the Una Vittoria hotel in Florence (Italy), designed by Fabio Novembre. *Summer Flowers*, Marco Braga's flowers and leaves décor on a beige background, looks like a tapestry. © Alberto Ferrero, 2003.
Detail of the wall of the Bar Lodi (Italy), a kind of tunnel sparkling with gold nuggets, "Sfumatura" collection, with a gradation of gold tesserae. The mirror-wall across the bar totally reflects it, thus doubling the space. © Alberto Ferrero, 1998.

A must of design, transformed into a giant sculpture, *La Poltrona di Proust Monumentale*, by Alessandro Mendini (2005). © Ottavio Tomasini, 2006.
Bathers at Asnières, Georges Seurat, 1884, 201 × 300 cm, National Gallery, London. Mendini has drawn his inspiration from this great theoretician of Pointilism. © National Gallery Company Limited, London.

Above: **Fabio Novembre**, then artistic director of Bisazza, at home under a mosaic snake by Sandro Chia. © Settimio Benedusi, 2005. Below: The designers **Marcel Wanders and Carlo Dal Bianco** inside Wander's funny polka-dot *Antelope* car. © Ottavio Tomasini, 2005. **The designer Isao Hosoe worked for Bisazza in 1995.** He is resting against one of the thick and curvaceous *Attore Spaziale 4* panels used to recreate space like a screen. © Marco Mignani, 1999.

The Coffee tables, magical pebbles created by Marcel Wanders for Bisazza. Here, the tesserae are meticulously recut by hand so as to fit their rounded shapes. Star of the avant-garde Droog group, Wanders also used the Bisazza mosaics in 2005 in suites of the Lute Suites hotel, near Amsterdam. © Ottavio Tomasini, 2005.

Design by Alessandro Mendini for the "Neomosaico" collection of 1998. A little classicism, lots of pop, a dash of new age, a bit of world music, and jazz galore. With Bisazza, small squares swing! © A. Mendini.
Detail of the Philosopher's Tower in Genova, during the 2004 Art & Architecture exhibition. Mendini covered its walls with several varicoloured patterns in Bisazza mosaics. © Ottavio Tomasini, 2004.

Fabio Novembre created for the Bisazza stand at the Bologna Cersaie a spiraled structure influenced by the Tatlin tower. © Alberto Ferrero, 2000.
Model of the monument dedicated by the constructivist sculptor Wladimir Tatlin to the Third International and exhibited in Moscow in 1920. A revolutionary work which inspired many 20th-century artists. © The Museum of Modern Art, New York/Scala photo, Florence.

The spectacular spiral staircase of the Groningen museum (Holland), designed by the Atelier Mendini. An example of the fruitful Mendini/Bisazza collaboration, which led to a new contemporary ornamental grammar, adaptable everywhere. © Mendini workshop, 1994.

Shimmering sequined dress by Azzedine Alaïa in the rooms of the Groningen museum during an Alaïa exhibition, in 1997. © Assouline.
Detail of the heart of the Mendini spiral staircase, a kind of gigantic kaleidoscope for the Groningen museum. Also made by the Atelier Mendini is the museum entrance hall, still with Bisazza tesserae. © Mendini workshop, 1994.

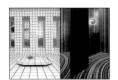

Music room of the tiled house created in 1979 by Jean-Pierre Raynaud, covered inside with white ceramic tiles. © Deidi Von Schaewen.
Stripes fall, a totally Bisazza atmosphere playing on the optical power of stripes, thanks to the *Oro* and *Gemme* tessera lines. A project by Fabio Novembre for the Berlin Bisazza showroom. © Alberto Ferrero, 2004.

Andrée Putman is a fervent adept of mosaic, especially in black and white... After decorating the Morgans hotel in New York, here she is, posing in the Pershing Hall in Paris, where the "Putman chic" consisted in daring to mix grey tesserae with golden aventurine tesserae. © André Rau/H&K.
Boxed book *The Putman Style*, edited by Assouline and covered with a grid of black and white Bisazza mosaics, like an object of the Viennese Secession, and in the spirit of perfection characteristic of Madame Putman. © Assouline.

Sculpted and gilt wooden armchair by Thomas Chippendale, 1764. The gold and the red silk of the seat and the massive aspect of its shape recall a throne. © V&A Images/Victoria and Albert Museum.
Evocation of a majestic Venice in this study room, with a *Damasco Rosso Oro* background décor. Bisazza knows how to draw his inspiration from the rarest brocades and the most lavish tapestries. Stylist: Michele Pasini/Storage © Federico Cedrone, 2005.

Photographs of sculptures by Antonio Canova, turned into giant black and white panels by means of 10 x 10 mm tesserae. Endimion's face invades the room, plunging the antique-like classicism into modernism. © Alberto Ferrero, 2003.
This 2,5 meter-high Hollywood Oscar is covered with hand-cut gold tesserae. It has been ornating the main building of the Academy of Motion Picture Arts and Sciences in Hollywood since 1998. © Bisazza.

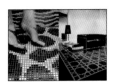

Like slender gazelle legs in the savannah, ravishing light feet graze the *Giraffa* mosaic floor with a *Zebra* décor background. Carlo Dal Bianco design. © Alberto Ferrero, 2003.
The juxtaposition of styles and humor typify the Bisazza spirit. The 1930s sofa by Le Corbusier/Charlotte Perriand/Pierre Jeanneret (reissued by Cassina), stands majestically on a trompe-l'œil carpet in the manner of a huge Thonet chair canework. Vienna Nero décor. Stylist: Michele Pasini/Storage. © Federico Cedrone, 2006.

Detail of the new Bisazza showroom in Milano, where the baroque is subtly counterbalanced by the design. Left, pillar covered with the *Winter Flowers Oro Nero* décor; center, *Giza Bianco* décor; above the Arne Jacobsen armchairs, the *Marie-Antoinette* chandelier. Carlo Dal Bianco design. Stylist : Michele Pasini/Storage. © Federico Cedrone, 2006.

Living Tower, a sculpture by the designer Verner Panton, 1969, 202 x 202 x 64 cm. © Bonhams, London, UK/The Bridgeman Art Library Nationality.
Entrance of the Lodi Bar, designed by Fabio Novembre in 1998. On the floor, trompe-l'œil silhouettes, meant to be the shadows of the shapes cut out in the mirror-wall across the bar. © Alberto Ferrero, 1998.

Bedroom with pearl reflections, with the baroque black lacquered bed standing out on a backdrop with giant silvery *Winter Flowers Oro Bianco*. Stylist: Michele Pasini/Storage © Federico Cedrone, 2005.
Flowery and bright atmosphere with white and gold shades at the Bisazza showroom in Milano. Another version of the large flower *Winter Flowers Oro Nero* tesserae. Stylist: Beatrice Rossetti. © Federico Cedrone, 2005.

The allure of a glamourous Grace Kelly-like style, worthy of the safaris in Hemingway's novels.... An African flavor with the *Giraffa* décor. Stylist: Miguel Arnau. © Giampaolo Sgura, 2004.

The highly sophisticated Tardini leather boutique in New York, designed by Fabio Novembre in 2003. The *Rettile* pattern creates the illusion of a huge snake-skin seen through a magnifying glass and covering the floor and the stand. Computer-made pattern. © Alberto Ferrero, 2003.

Detail of the *China Birds Brown* décor created by Marco Braga, 2005. This journey to an imaginary East can also be accomplished by using various shades of blue, cobalt among them. © Bisazza.

Let yourself be caught red-handed with the bags of the New York Tardini boutique! Real alligator or fake snake, the choice is yours in this troubling, sensuous and dizzying atmosphere. © Alberto Ferrero, 2003.

This huge *Pot pour le Cèdre* by Alessandro Mendini shines since 2002 in the garden of the Cartier Foundation for Contemporary Art, in Paris. It was brought there for the "Fragilisme" exhibition. © Alberto Ferrero, 2002.

Anna Molinari's Blumarine boutique in London, designed by Fabio Novembre in 1994. Two long golden legs open onto a red grotto atmosphere lit by blue neon lights. © Alberto Ferrero, 1994.

Contemporary chinoiserie designed by Muriel Brandolini for a refined Manhattan bachelor. © Pieter Estersohn, photograph originally published in *House & Garden*.

Coral, transformed by Marco Braga for Bisazza; the branches even intermesh and climb on the wall, which shimmers thanks to the mixture of white glass and gold tesserae. © Bisazza.

Hall of the New York Bisazza showroom created by Fabio Novembre in 2003. This free, three-dimensional interpretation of the gardens designed by the architect Palladio in the 16th century is stunning. It spectacularly redivides space by means of volutes. © Alberto Ferrero, 2003. *Nu Bleu II* by Henri Matisse, 1952, 1162 x 889 cm. Musée national d'art moderne Centre Pompidou, Paris. © Henri Matisse heirs; photograph: CNAC/MNAM Dist. RMN/DR.

Andy Warhol in his mythical workshop office at the Factory, in New York. In the 1960s, his assistants reproduced, almost as on an assembly line, the *Flowers* series—gigantic and flat images of stylized, very pop flowers. © Ugo Mulas stat.

The big *Fiore Blu* blue flowers, reminiscent of Warhol, Matisse or, even, aloha prints, cover the bottom of this swimming pool. © Bisazza, 2005.

Sparkling bathroom with, behind the shower, a wall entirely done with *Sfumatura Gladiolo*, accentuating the impression of the shimmer of the water. Stylist: Michele Pasini/Storage. © Federico Cedrone, 2005.

Charming outside shower on a field of white daisies; *Pratoline 8* décor, with the very weatherproof *Opus Romano* tesserae. Stylist: Beatrice Rossetti. © Federico Cedrone, 2005.

Staircase forming sentences from Samuel Beckett's play *Waiting For Godot*. A Fabio Novembre project for the Bisazza showroom in Berlin. © Alberto Ferrero, 2004. Could this model be waiting for Godot? A perfect illustration of the made-in-Bisazza humor with black, gold, white and yellow 12 x 12 mm tesserae. © Alberto Ferrero, 2004.

Detail from the *Springrose Nero* collection. Entire walls can be covered with these huge roses on a black background, thus creating a stunning tapestry effect.Design: Carlo Dal Bianco. © Bisazza. Right: The main entrance hall of the Bisazza headquarters, in Alte, is very much like today's firm, mixing tradition and innovation. The small, 1 cm² tesserae form a spectacular, giant rose garden on a black backdrop. Stylist: Barbara Guidoni/Storage. © Alberto Ferrero, 2003.

Invitation to meditation, before the trompe-l'œil, on the *Montparnasse* panel, of a fire crackling in a fireplace, reclining in the comfortable Charles Eames's *Lounge Chair*, "Bisazza Home" collection. Design: Marco Braga. © Federico Cedrone, 2006.

The publisher wishes to thank Piero Bisazza, Rossella Bisazza, Jeanne Boyer, Véronique Massuger and Elisabeth Védrenne. Thanks are also due: to Mrs Andrée Putman and Jean-Pierre Raynaud; to the designers/artists: Marco Braga, Sandro Chia, Carlo Dal Bianco, Isao Hosoe, Javier Mariscal, Alessandro Mendini, Fabio Novembre, Oscar Tusquets, Patricia Urquiola, Marcel Wanders; to the photographers: Settimio Benedusi, Federico Cedrone, Pieter Estersohn for *House & Garden*, Alberto Ferrero, Marco Mignani, Ugo Mulas, Deidi Von Schaewen, Gianpaolo Sgura et Ottavio Tomasini; to the stylists: Miguel Arnau, Barbara Ghidoni Storage, Michele Pasini Storage and Beatrice Rossetti; to The Bridgeman Art Library, Valentina Bandelloni (Scala Archives), Valentina Balzarotti Barbieri et Stefania Cattaneo (Agenzia Letteraria Internazionale), Eitan Fisher (Pieter Estersohn Photography), Gwenaelle Fossard (Succession Henri Matisse), Stéphane Gerschel (Archives Andrée Putman), Laurence Kersuzan et Pierrick Jan (RMN), Rebecca Staffolani (Picture Library, The National Gallery, Londres).